UGANDA 2016 HUMAN RIGHTS REPORT

EXECUTIVE SUMMARY

Uganda is a constitutional republic led since 1986 by President Yoweri Museveni of the National Resistance Movement (NRM) party. On February 18, voters re-elected Museveni to a fifth five-year term and returned an NRM majority to the unicameral National Assembly. The elections fell short of international standards and were marred by allegations of disenfranchisement and voter intimidation, harassment of the opposition, closure of social media websites, and lack of transparency and independence in the Electoral Commission.

Civilian authorities generally maintained effective control over the security forces.

The three most serious human rights problems in the country included lack of respect for individual integrity (unlawful killings, torture, arbitrary detention, and other abuse of suspects and detainees); restrictions on civil liberties (freedoms of press, expression, assembly, association, and political participation); and violence and discrimination against marginalized groups, such as women, children, persons with disabilities, and the lesbian, gay, bisexual, transgender, and intersex (LGBTI) community.

Other human rights problems included harsh prison conditions, lengthy pretrial detention, official corruption, biased application of the law, societal violence, trafficking in persons, and child labor.

The government was reluctant to investigate, prosecute, or punish officials who committed human rights violations, whether in the security services or elsewhere in government, and impunity was a problem.

Section 1. Respect for the Integrity of the Person, Including Freedom from:

a. Arbitrary Deprivation of Life and other Unlawful or Politically Motivated Killings

There were several reports the government or its agents committed arbitrary or unlawful killings, including as a result of torture.

Media outlets reported that, on November 26 and 27 in Kasese District, the Uganda People's Defense Forces (UPDF) and Uganda Police Force (UPF) killed between

60 and 250 persons, including unarmed civilians, during clashes with supporters of Charles Wesley Mumbere, the Rwenzururu king. According to the UPF, on November 26, the king's royal guards attacked an unspecified number of police stations in Rwenzori Region, resulting in the deaths of 14 police officers; 41 royal guards also were killed. The following day security forces reportedly stormed the palace and arrested the king after he failed to comply with a UPDF order to surrender his royal guards to the military. According to unconfirmed reports, security forces killed women and children who were on the compound during the raid, and several bodies were found with bound hands, possibly indicating victims had submitted to arrest before being killed. Amnesty International reported that "many people appeared to have been summarily shot and their bodies dumped." One international organization alleged security forces made no attempt to minimize civilian casualties, an assertion security forces did not dispute.

UPDF officers claimed soldiers fired in self-defense after royal guards attacked them with machetes, bows and arrows, and spears. Civil society and international organizations claimed the government's disproportionate use of force was unjustified and that the Rwenzururu Kingdom presented no immediate security threat. The government claimed the kingdom had militant secessionist ambitions, which forced it to take immediate and definitive action.

In addition to the king, 139 royal guards were arrested and charged with murder, terrorism, and treason. On December 15, media published images of the guards at their initial hearing, where defense lawyers asserted their visible injuries resulted from torture. Media reported the president ordered a parliamentary committee tasked with investigating the raid to stop its investigation. The Uganda Human Rights Commission (UHRC) had not completed its investigation into the raid by year's end. Trials of the king and his guards continued at year's end.

On October 17, media reported game rangers attached to the Uganda Wildlife Authority (UWA) killed seven unarmed, suspected poachers. Reports asserted the park rangers facilitated the poachers' hunts in exchange for a portion of the revenue and then killed the seven for failing to pay the rangers their promised share. The UWA denied its staff was involved in the killings and said the UPF was investigating.

Local leaders and civil society organizations reported that police had yet to take action against officers who in September 2015 allegedly shot and killed five persons in Apaa Parish in the north. The killings occurred during a land dispute related to the government's border demarcation.

There were no known developments in the investigation into the African Union's August 2015 indictment of three UPDF soldiers for their alleged role in the July 2015 killing of seven civilians at a wedding party in Marka, Somalia. Media reported the killings occurred following a bomb attack on an African Union Mission in Somalia convoy.

b. Disappearance

There were no reports of politically motivated disappearances during the year.

Following the December 2015 disappearance of Christopher Aine--campaign aide to Amama Mbabazi, a former prime minister and presidential candidate--police offered a reward of 20 million shillings ($5,700) for information on his whereabouts, ostensibly to question him about his involvement in a clash between President Museveni's supporters and security team. On April 7, a local television station aired footage of Aine with General Caleb Akandwanaho (aka Salim Saleh), the president's brother, and a senior advisor at a Kampala hotel. Aine said he had fled to Tanzania in December 2015 to escape harassment and intimidation by state security operatives.

c. Torture and Other Cruel, Inhuman, or Degrading Treatment or Punishment

The constitution and law prohibit such practices. The 2012 Antitorture Act stipulates that any person convicted of an act of torture may be subject to 15 years' imprisonment, a fine of 7.2 million shillings ($2,050), or both. The penalty for conviction of aggravated torture is life imprisonment. Nevertheless, there were credible reports security forces tortured and beat suspects.

From January to June, the African Center for Treatment and Rehabilitation of Torture Victims (ACTV) registered 856 allegations of torture by police, the Flying Squad (a UPF unit assigned to violent crimes), special investigations units of police, and the UPDF. The ACTV provided legal advice to 142 torture victims and initiated three public litigation cases of torture against the government.

The ACTV reported that Twaha Kasaija, whom marine police arrested for theft on March 23, was tortured to death at Walukuba Police Station. According to the ACTV, Kasaija's injuries suggested he was punched, kicked, and beaten with batons, wire cable, and sticks. Kasaija's brother, Abdul Rahman Muyima, and neighbor, Mohammed Kitakule, also were arrested and appeared to have been beaten with batons, wire cable, and sticks. Police arrested officers Patrick Katete and Charles Okure (the officer in charge) but later released Okure on bond; Katete remained in jail awaiting trial on murder charges at year's end.

The UHRC reported it awarded 36.6 million shillings ($10,450) in compensation to victims of torture and other abuses from January through June.

Prison and Detention Center Conditions

Prison conditions remained poor and, in some cases, life threatening. Serious problems included overcrowding, physical abuse of detainees by security staff and fellow inmates, inadequate food, and understaffing. Local human rights groups, including the ACTV, received reports of torture by security forces and prison personnel. Reports of forced labor continued. Most prisons did not have accommodations for persons with disabilities.

Physical Conditions: Gross overcrowding remained a problem. According to the Uganda Prisons Service (UPS), the prison system had a maximum inmate capacity of 22,000 but incarcerated 48,689. The Foundation for Human Rights Initiative (FHRI), which had visited 13 police stations and 13 prisons by August, reported that four of the five prisons in the north were particularly overcrowded. Gulu Prison, for example, held 1,400 inmates in a facility designed for 400. Prison authorities blamed the overcrowding on the criminal justice system's inability to process cases in a timely manner.

As of August, 233 babies stayed in prison with their mothers. Some women's prisons also had day-care facilities. Authorities in Kampala separated pretrial detainees from convicted prisoners, but prisons in other areas did not.

The UPS reported 67 inmate deaths between January and August. Causes of death included malaria, cardiac arrest, anemia, pneumonia, and tuberculosis. Media reported deaths also occurred as a result of suicide and police abuse.

In interviews with prisoners, FHRI received reports of prison staff and fellow inmates beating and abusing prisoners, although there were fewer such reports than in previous years. In Koboko Prison, for example, guards reportedly assigned certain inmates leadership positions and gave them sticks, which they often used to beat fellow prisoners.

The UHRC inspected 106 of the country's 247 prisons and four military detention facilities during the year. It found that prisons in Koboko and Nebbi districts did not have health centers, requiring inmates to walk long distances, under guard, to access medical care. Outside Kampala, some prisons lacked sufficient food, water, medical care, means to transport inmates to court, bedding, infrastructure, and sanitation facilities.

Provision of food and medical services in jails also was inadequate. According to detainees and guards at the 13 police stations FHRI had visited by August, detainees received only one meal per day. According to the UHRC, which inspected 183 of 300 police stations during the year, some stations did not provide meals to suspects and most lacked the means to transport suspects to court.

Administration: Recordkeeping remained a problem. The UPS claimed it was unable to manage information because it lacked computers.

The UPS reported that its assistant commissioner in charge of human rights investigated and mediated complaints between management and prisoners. The UPS added that each prison had a human rights committee responsible for addressing complaints and relaying them to the assistant commissioner. Prison authorities acknowledged a backlog in the investigation of complaints.

Independent Monitoring: Authorities allowed FHRI and the ACTV to conduct prison visits with advance notification. The International Committee of the Red Cross declined to comment on whether it conducted prison visits during the year.

Improvements: During the year prison authorities hired 1,548 new staff--mainly wardens, cadet principal officers, and cadet assistant superintendents of prisons-- increasing the total number of UPS staff to 7,448. The UPS acknowledged, however, that it still had a staff shortage of 5,000. The UPS also installed flush toilets in 47 of the 58 prisons, constructed four new prisons, and renovated two others. Unlike in the previous year, women had separate facilities in all prisons. The UPS had a budget to accommodate pregnant women and mothers with infants, and pregnant mothers received antenatal care services and special diets.

d. Arbitrary Arrest or Detention

Although the constitution and law prohibit such practices, security forces often arbitrarily arrested and detained persons, including opposition leaders, politicians, activists, demonstrators, and journalists.

Role of the Police and Security Apparatus

Under the Ministry of Internal Affairs, the UPF has primary responsibility for law enforcement. The UPDF, under the Ministry of Defense, is responsible for external security and may aid civil authorities when responding to riots or other disturbances of the peace. The Chieftaincy of Military Intelligence is legally under UPDF authority and may detain civilians suspected of rebel or terrorist activity. Other agencies with law enforcement powers include the Directorate of Counter Terrorism, Joint Intelligence Committee, and Special Forces Brigade, among others.

The UPF reported its ability to perform its law enforcement duties was constrained by limited resources, including low pay and lack of vehicles, equipment, and training. The UPF's Professional Standards Unit investigated complaints of police abuse, including torture, assault, unlawful arrest and detention, death in custody, mismanagement of case documentation, and corrupt practices. Police continued to use excessive force, including torture, and impunity was a problem (see sections 1.a. and 1.c.).

Between January and August, police ignored the instruction of the director of public prosecution (DPP) to add Aaron Baguma, former commander of Kampala's Central Police Station, to the list of suspected accomplices in the October 2015 killing of Donah Katusabe, a Kampala businessperson. On August 30, 12 days after the court issued an arrest warrant for Baguma, he turned himself in and was charged with murder, kidnapping with intent to murder, and robbery. The court, which remanded him to Kigo Prison, subsequently released him on bail. The case continued at year's end.

Police and soldiers not only failed to prevent societal violence, they sometimes targeted opposition supporters. For example, on July 12 and 13, media broadcast videos of police, soldiers, and plainclothes officers using sticks to beat unarmed supporters of the main opposition leader, Kizza Besigye, as his car passed on a Kampala street; they also beat motorcycle taxi drivers who appeared uninvolved in Besigye's procession. In one instance a police truck veered onto a sidewalk to hit from behind and knock over a man waving at Besigye's passing vehicle. Police arrested Benon Matsiko, an officer, for allegedly driving the truck, noting he would face internal disciplinary measures; Matsiko denied he was the driver. Another man--who media members subsequently identified as Yusuf Lubowa, a member of a progovernment civilian group called Bodaboda 2010--then kicked the fallen man in the same knee struck by the vehicle. Although media reports showed that Lubowa had participated in multiple police operations against Besigye supporters, the UPF claimed it did not know him. Police initiated an internal disciplinary proceeding and charged five officers and four commanders with unlawful exercise of authority and discrediting the reputation of police. There was no known update on these cases by the end of the year.

Private lawyers separately filed a criminal case against Inspector General of Police (IGP) Kale Kayihura and seven senior commanders, accusing them of torture for their role in the July 12 and 13 beatings. On July 21, a magistrate's court issued criminal summonses for IGP Kayihura and the seven senior police officers to appear on August 10 for arraignment on charges of torture. According to the private prosecution lawyers, the officers refused to receive the summonses, and none appeared in court. On August 26, Deputy Chief Justice Steven Kavuma halted the criminal case against Kayihura and the other officers, stating the case could not proceed until the court resolved NRM Youth League member Robert Rutaro's petition that challenged the court's authority to try the IGP as a private citizen for actions he took in his institutional role. By year's end, the court had not resolved the petition.

The UHRC reported it provided human rights training to 232 security officials in police and district administrations of Fort Portal, Mbarara, and Arua districts.

The UPF reported that it opened an unspecified number of new community police stations to expand its community policing operations. In 2015 it authorized civilians to police their respective communities as "crime preventers." Crime preventers, nominally under the authority of district police commanders, received one to two months of training and have arrest authority. While estimates of their number varied, the IGP claimed there were 11 million crime preventers nationwide, equating to approximately one-third of the country's population. UPF officials stated they intended to place 30 crime preventers in each village in the country. Media and civil society reports accused crime preventers of human rights abuses. On April 18, for example, the chief administrative officer of Lira District said his office had received many reports of crime preventers involved in rape, arbitrary arrests, and torture.

Arrest Procedures and Treatment of Detainees

The law requires that judges or prosecutors issue a warrant before an arrest is made, unless the arrest is made during commission of a crime or while in pursuit of

a perpetrator. Nevertheless, authorities often arrested suspects without warrants.
The law requires authorities to charge suspects within 48 hours of arrest, but they
frequently held suspects longer without charge. Authorities must try suspects
arrested under the Antiterrorism Law within 120 days (360 days if charged with a
capital offense) or release them on bail; if the case is presented to the court before
the expiration of this period, there is no limit on further pretrial detention. While
the law requires authorities to inform detainees immediately of the reasons for
detention, at times they did not do so. The law provides for bail at the discretion of
the judge, but many suspects were unaware of the law. Judges generally granted
requests for bail. The law provides detainees the right to legal representation and
access to a lawyer; but this right often was not respected. The law requires the
government to provide an attorney for indigent defendants charged with capital
offenses. Citizens detained without charge may file civil suit against the Attorney
General's Office for compensation for unlawful detention. Security forces held
suspects, particularly opposition leaders, incommunicado and under house arrest.

Arbitrary Arrest: Arbitrary arrests, particularly of opposition leaders, remained a
problem. Police often carried out "preventative arrests" for alleged treason and
incitement of violence.

On February 24, the day of local government elections, police detained opposition
candidate Besigye at his home, effectively denying him the right to vote.
Following the February elections, police intermittently placed Besigye under 10-
day house arrests. Police reportedly confined him to his home for the entire month
of March, releasing him on April 1, the day the Supreme Court validated the
president's electoral victory. Despite widespread media and nongovernmental
organization (NGO) reporting, the UPF repeatedly denied Besigye was under
house arrest, and the IGP claimed police were merely "closely monitoring
Besigye's movements." Media reported that on May 5, police resumed Besigye's
house arrest and confined Kampala's opposition-affiliated mayor, Erias Lukwago,
and opposition chief whip Ibrahim Ssemujju Nganda to their homes.

On May 11, Besigye eluded police surveillance at his home and drove to
Kampala's city center, where he was filmed taking a mock presidential oath of
office in front of a crowd of protesters. Police arrested Besigye and flew him to
the remote Karamoja Region in the northeast, where they detained him at the
Moroto Police Station. Two days later, Besigye was charged with treason and
remanded to Moroto Prison. On May 16, he was transferred to Luzira Prison in
Kampala after defense lawyers and his family asked for a transfer. He remained in

detention until July 12, when the court released him on bail. Besigye's treason case continued at year's end.

Pretrial Detention: Case backlogs due to an inefficient judiciary that lacked adequate funding and staff, the absence of plea bargaining prior to 2015, and insufficient use of bail contributed to pretrial detentions as long as seven years. The UPS reported 55 percent of inmates were pretrial detainees. The judiciary introduced a plea bargaining mechanism at High Court circuits across the country in 2015 after a successful pilot program in 2014.

FHRI reported police arrested Moses Tumusime in 2008 on murder charges. He last appeared in court in 2008 and remained in custody in Kitalya Prison. In November the officer in charge of the prison reported Tumusime was still held on remand and that his file was sent to the High Court in 2012.

Detainee's Ability to Challenge Lawfulness of Detention before a Court: Persons arrested have the right to file a legal challenge against their detention and obtain prompt release and compensation if a judge determines the detention to have been unlawful. This mechanism was seldom employed and rarely successful.

Amnesty: Since 2000 the government has offered blanket unconditional amnesty for all crimes committed by individuals who engaged in war or armed rebellion against the government, barring grave breaches of the Geneva Convention, genocide, willful killings of innocent civilians, and other serious crimes perpetrated against civilians or communities without military necessity.

e. Denial of Fair Public Trial

The constitution and law provide for an independent judiciary, but the government did not always respect this provision. Corruption, understaffing, inefficiency, and executive branch interference with judicial rulings often undermined the courts' independence.

The president appoints Supreme Court, Court of Appeal, and High Court judges and members of the Judicial Service Commission (which makes recommendations on appointments to the judiciary) with the approval of the National Assembly.

Due to vacancies on the Supreme Court, Constitutional Court, High Court, and the lower courts, the judiciary did not deliver justice in a timely manner. At times the lack of judicial quorum precluded cases from proceeding.

Judicial corruption was a problem. The Center for Public Interest Law (CEPIL) reported in August that judicial corruption mainly consisted of cash bribes to clerks and magistrates for favorable treatment. CEPIL noted that instances of corruption in the lower courts were more visible and egregious as magistrates openly contravened court rules to favor one party. In the higher courts (High Court, Court of Appeal, and Supreme Court), corruption was more discreet and nuanced. Media reported several incidents of police arresting lower court judicial officers for allegedly soliciting bribes, while there were no such arrests of higher court officials. CEPIL's report noted that "systemic corruption within the justice system undermines human rights and public confidence."

Trial Procedures

Although the law provides for a presumption of innocence, authorities did not always respect this right. Defendants have the right to be informed promptly and in detail of the charges and have free interpretation from the moment charged through all appeals, as necessary. An inadequate system of judicial administration resulted in a serious backlog of cases, undermining suspects' right to a speedy trial. Defendants have the right to be present at their trial and to consult with an attorney of their choice. The law requires the government to provide an attorney for indigent defendants accused of capital offenses. Defendants have the right to adequate time and facilities to prepare a defense and appeal, with free interpretation as necessary. Defendants have the right to obtain evidence the state intends to use prior to their trial, although this right of disclosure is not absolute in sensitive cases, and authorities did not always respect this right. The law allows defendants to confront or question witnesses testifying against them and present witnesses and evidence on their own behalf, but authorities did not always respect this right. Defendants may not be compelled to testify or confess guilt, and they have the right to appeal. These rights extended to all groups.

All nonmilitary trials are public. A single judge decides cases in the High Court, while a panel of at least five judges decides cases in the constitutional and supreme courts. The law allows military courts to try civilians that assist members of the military in committing offenses or are found possessing arms, ammunition, or other equipment reserved for the armed forces. On September 16, the High Court ruled that member of parliament (MP) Michael Kabaziguruka, who was charged with treason along with 26 military officers, would be tried by a military court.

Political Prisoners and Detainees

During the year authorities detained numerous opposition politicians and activists on politically motivated grounds. Authorities released many without charge but charged others with crimes including terrorism, treason, inciting violence, holding illegal meetings, and abuse of office. No statistics on the number of political detainees or prisoners were available.

There was no available information on whether the government permitted international human rights or humanitarian organizations access to political detainees.

On February 29, the Forum for Democratic Change (FDC) claimed security force personnel had arrested and detained approximately 300 of its supporters nationwide over the course of the election season. The UPF claimed it had arrested 132 persons from various political parties for illegal election-related activities.

On June 8 and 13, police arrested Michael Kabaziguruka, an MP and FDC deputy commissioner on the Electoral Commission, and released him within two days of each arrest. On June 26, police rearrested Kabaziguruka and subsequently transferred him to Kigo Prison, where he awaited trial at year's end. On June 28, a military court charged Kabaziguruka and 26 others, predominantly military officers, with treason for allegedly plotting the violent overthrow of the government. According to Kabaziguruka's lawyers, the government based its most recent charges on the same evidence as it used for its 2012 treason case against Kabaziguruka and three other individuals, a case the government dropped. On July 1, in a meeting with opposition politicians, the president accused Kabaziguruka of attempting to assassinate him. On September 16, the High Court ruled that Kabaziguruka be tried in a military court; Kabaziguruka appealed.

Civil Judicial Procedures and Remedies

There is an independent and impartial judiciary in civil matters. Victims may report cases of human rights violations through the regular court system or the UHRC, which has judicial powers under the constitution. These powers include the authority to order the release of detainees, pay compensation to victims, and pursue other legal and administrative remedies, such as mediation. Victims may appeal their cases to the Court of Appeal and thereafter to the Supreme Court but not to an international or regional court. Civil courts and the UHRC have no ability to hold perpetrators of human rights abuses criminally liable, and bureaucratic delays hampered enforcement of judgments that granted financial compensation.

f. Arbitrary or Unlawful Interference with Privacy, Family, Home, or Correspondence

The constitution and law prohibit such actions, but there were reports the government failed to respect these prohibitions. Police did not always obtain search warrants to enter private homes and offices.

The Antiterrorism Act and the Regulation of Interception of Communications Bill authorize government security agencies to tap private conversations to combat terrorism-related offenses. The government utilized both statutes to monitor telephone and internet communications.

The government encouraged university students and government officials, including members of the judiciary, to attend NRM political education and military science courses known as "chaka mchaka." While the government claimed the courses were not compulsory, human rights activists and opposition politicians reported authorities pressured civil servants and students to attend.

Section 2. Respect for Civil Liberties, Including:

a. Freedom of Speech and Press

The constitution and law provide for freedom of speech and press, but the government often restricted these rights.

Freedom of Speech and Expression: The government restricted opposition political parties from speaking to the press, and police detained activists who publicly criticized the government.

On February 19 and May 9, police raided FDC party headquarters, fired tear gas, blocked entry to the offices, and cancelled scheduled press conferences. According to media reports on February 19, an officer on the scene claimed police sealed the site because of reasonable suspicion the party was planning criminal activity. On May 9, police arrested FDC deputy secretary general Harold Kaija while he addressed a press conference. According to media, a police spokesperson stated that police arrested Kaija "as he attempted to address a press conference on a parallel swearing-in ceremony" for former presidential candidate Besigye, which had been organized by the FDC to parody the official ceremony set for May 12.

<u>Press and Media Freedoms</u>: The country had an active media environment with numerous privately owned newspapers and television and radio stations. These media outlets regularly covered stories and often provided commentary critical of the government and officials. The UPF's Media Crimes Unit, however, closely monitored all radio, television, and print media, and security forces subjected numerous journalists to harassment, intimidation, and arrest. Government officials and ruling party members owned many of the private rural radio stations and imposed reporting restrictions.

Cabinet minister Mwesigwa Rukutana, who owned Radio Ankole in Ntungamo District, directed his staff not to broadcast advertisements placed by independent and opposition politicians during the election season.

<u>Violence and Harassment</u>: Security forces assaulted journalists. For example, on May 24, media reported that Abraham James Byandala, then minister without portfolio, punched a journalist in the abdomen as she was covering a court case in which he was charged with corruption. The journalist filed a complaint against the minister but subsequently withdrew it.

Security forces also arbitrarily arrested journalists. For example, local media reported that, on February 22, a plainclothes police officer pepper-sprayed the eyes of freelance photojournalist Isaac Kasamani while he was covering police confinement of opposition leader Besigye to his home (see section 1.d.). On February 27, police arrested Eriasa Sserunjogi and Abubaker Lubowa, journalists working for opposition-leaning newspaper *Daily Monitor,* who also were covering the Besigye house arrest. Police detained the two journalists at Kasangati Police Station for several hours before releasing them without charge.

Security forces also harassed and intimidated journalists. On January 10, for example, media reported police in Moroto, in the northeast, confiscated and destroyed journalists' cameras to stop them from filming a roadblock erected to stop Besigye from traveling to a campaign event. Regional police commander Richard Aruk condemned the action and advised the journalists to file a complaint to enable his office to investigate the incident.

Police also arbitrarily detained foreign journalists. On February 7, police arrested two BBC journalists filming outside Abim Hospital in the northeast. The district police commander claimed they had no permission from the Ministry of Health to film at the hospital. Police released the journalists that night without charge.

On November 27, police detained Kenya Television Network reporter and anchor Joy Doreen Biira for "abetting terrorism" after she reported on the UPF and UPDF's November 27 raid on the Rwenzururu king's palace (see section 1.a.). The Committee to Protect Journalists stated, "It is bad enough that Ugandan authorities desired to censor coverage of a newsworthy event, but the use of antiterrorism laws to intimidate a journalist is a vast overreach." Police released Biira the following day and she was allowed to return to Kenya. Police have not yet charged Biira but claim to be investigating her case.

<u>Censorship or Content Restrictions</u>: The government directly and indirectly restricted media coverage and content.

On December 6, for example, the Uganda Communications Commission (UCC) prohibited further media reporting on the November 27 raid by security forces on the Rwenzururu king's palace, claiming it could influence an ongoing court case.

In response to the attorney general's April 28 petition to the Constitutional Court, which claimed the opposition-led civil unrest campaign "Defiance" was an unconstitutional effort to stop the lawful swearing-in ceremony of the president, the Constitutional Court the same day issued a one-month prohibition on activities by the campaign to allow sufficient time for the court to review the attorney general's petition. On May 5, citing the court ruling, Minister for Information Jim Muhwezi stated that the government would revoke the license of any media house that covered any aspect or activity of the Defiance campaign. Although the swearing-in ceremony took place on May 12, the court had not set a date to hear the petition by year's end, nor had the attorney general requested an extension of the prohibition.

Many print and broadcast journalists practiced self-censorship, particularly when reporting on the president or his inner circle.

<u>Libel/Slander Laws</u>: Authorities used libel and slander laws to suppress criticism of government officials.

On April 21, the police Criminal Investigations Directorate questioned *Daily Monitor* journalists Alex Atuhaire and Yasiin Mugerwa concerning alleged criminal libel. The questioning focused on an article reporting statements by members of the Rwenzori Region's parliament accusing a cabinet minister of inciting postelection violence.

Internet Freedom

The government cited security as justification to restrict and disrupt internet access, especially to social media sites.

On February 17, the UCC ordered telecommunication companies to block user access to Facebook, Twitter, WhatsApp, and mobile phone financial transaction services on February 18, election day. The UCC claimed it had evidence of plans to use these sites to foment unrest and violence. The affected sites were inaccessible for almost three days.

On May 11, again citing security, the UCC ordered telecommunications companies to disable access to social media for more than 24 hours while international dignitaries attended the president's fifth inauguration ceremony.

Citing the Antiterrorism Act, the Regulation of Interception of Communications Bill, and the Computer Misuse Act, the government monitored internet communication. According to the UCC, approximately 37 percent of the population used the internet.

The case of Robert Shaka, who was arrested and released on bail in June 2015 for allegedly violating the president's privacy by posting statements about his health on Facebook, continued.

Academic Freedom and Cultural Events

The government occasionally restricted academic freedom and cultural events. Authorities blocked retired Supreme Court justice George Kanyeihamba, a former NRM loyalist turned critic, from addressing Makerere University law students on the February elections. The Human Rights and Peace Center (HURIPEC) reported government officials also influenced academic appointments at public universities on the basis of political affiliation.

HURIPEC reported government officials attempted to prohibit, censor, cancel, or restrict films and musical presentations that addressed political themes or criticized the administration. Officials unsuccessfully attempted to ban Robert Kyagulanyi's song Ddembe ("Liberty"), which called for peaceful elections and transfer of power. Media reported the Uganda Broadcasting Corporation declined to air the song, and officials directed radio program directors not to play it. The UCC denied the government had banned the song. HURIPEC also reported the government banned a free DVD about the country's history, which was widely distributed on Kampala's streets. Police deemed its possession a crime for its "inappropriate and violent content."

b. Freedom of Peaceful Assembly and Association

Freedom of Assembly

While the constitution provides for freedom of assembly, the government did not respect this right. The government used the 2013 Public Order Management Act (POMA) to limit the right to assemble, especially for political opponents and critics of the government. The act places a significant bureaucratic burden on those wishing to organize or host gatherings and affords the UPF wide discretion to prevent or disrupt gatherings.

During and after the presidential election, UPF officers disrupted scheduled opposition rallies and meetings, even in some cases when authorities had granted permission. In many instances, the UPF provided no official response to requests to hold public meetings.

In two separate incidents on February 15, the final day of the presidential campaign, UPF officers prevented Besigye from appearing at campaign rallies approved by the Electoral Commission by blocking his access. Police fired teargas to disperse supporters who had gathered at the rally sites. During both incidents police arrested Besigye before releasing him without charge. Media reported that, during the second incident, police also fired bullets to disperse the crowd, resulting in one civilian death.

On February 19, a day after the elections, police arrested senior FDC officials, blockaded their party headquarters, and cancelled a scheduled FDC press conference. When FDC supporters gathered at party headquarters to protest, police reportedly fired tear gas and bullets to disperse the crowd and arrested eight supporters.

After the elections the UPF cited its legal powers of "preventive arrest," which allow police to remove and detain persons to prevent them from committing a crime and the POMA to harass opposition leaders. Police "preventively" arrested several opposition leaders attempting to hold meetings and other events, generally releasing them the same day. Police often prevented Besigye and other opposition leaders from participating in political events by confining them to their residences. When police allowed Besigye to leave his home, they often arrested him to prevent him from meeting with supporters or party officials. FHRI reported that, on February 22, police arrested Besigye and remanded him to the Naggalama Police Station after he attempted to go to the Electoral Commission to collect forms to contest the election results. According to IGP Kayihura, Besigye's intent was to rally supporters and cause chaos in the city, in violation of the POMA.

In response to the FDC's "Free My Vote" campaign, which called for an independent audit of presidential election results, police often disbanded peaceful protest meetings, including prayer groups, and arrested protest organizers.

In response to the FDC's May 5 call for nationwide protests to contest the outcome of the presidential election, the head of the Constitutional Court, Deputy Chief Justice Steven Kavuma, issued an order prohibiting the FDC from organizing "demonstrations, processions, other public meetings, media campaigns or pronouncements including but not limited to planned demonstrations or processions scheduled for May 5 or any other day among other orders." On May 6, media reported police had arrested 88 opposition supporters for participating in banned demonstrations.

Freedom of Association

While the constitution and law provide for freedom of association, the government did not always respect this right. On January 30, the president signed the NGO Act passed by the National Assembly in November 2015. The law includes a clause that requires NGOs to receive approval from local NGO monitoring committees, local governments, and relevant line ministries in each district in which they operate to be registered and active. The law also prohibits NGOs from engaging in acts "prejudicial to the interests of Uganda and the dignity of the people of Uganda." Discriminatory aspects of the law prevented LGBTI organizations from registering as NGOs.

The NGO Board, under the Ministry of Internal Affairs, regulates NGO activities and approves their registrations. It is composed of representatives from various ministries, including the security services.

FHRI reported that during the year intruders broke into various NGO offices, taking computers, files, and other sources of information. The nature of the crimes, along with limited police action to pursue perpetrators, led some of the affected organizations to suspect government involvement. In a May 22 incident, closed-circuit television (CCTV) footage showed four unidentified intruders breaking into the Kampala office of the Human Rights Awareness and Promotion Forum (HRAPF), which provides legal support for sexual minorities. The next morning, HRAPF staff found the dead body of the guard on duty at the time of the break-in, along with documents, a television screen, and keys, on the organization's compound. Police arrived at the scene two hours after HRAPF reported the incident, but no investigation had been initiated by year's end.

On April 10, according to Human Rights Network for Journalists (HRNJ) staff, a late evening female visitor to HRNJ's Kampala office offered the security guard food laced with sedatives. CCTV footage showed four men entering the premises and ransacking them after the guard apparently had passed out.

c. Freedom of Religion

See the Department of State's *International Religious Freedom Report* at www.state.gov/religiousfreedomreport/.

d. Freedom of Movement, Internally Displaced Persons, Protection of Refugees, and Stateless Persons

The constitution and law provide for freedom of internal movement, foreign travel, emigration, and repatriation.

The government cooperated with the Office of the UN High Commissioner for Refugees (UNHCR) and other humanitarian organizations in providing protection and assistance to internally displaced persons, refugees, returning refugees, asylum seekers, stateless persons, and other persons of concern.

Protection of Refugees

Access to Asylum: The law provides for the granting of asylum or refugee status, and the government has an established system for providing protection to refugees. The government has consistently provided a safe haven for refugees and asylum seekers. As of November 1, UNHCR, in partnership with the government, had identified an estimated 898,000 refugees and asylum seekers of different nationalities. Of these, 270,000 were from the Democratic Republic of the Congo and 476,000 from South Sudan. Other countries of origin included Burundi, Somalia, Rwanda, and Eritrea. The government provided adequate protection to refugees, including temporary protection, resettlement, and other long-term solutions.

As of July there were 39,000 asylum seekers in the country. According to UNHCR, the government made little progress in clearing the backlog because the Refugee Appeals Board has not operated since 2014.

The government did not fulfill UNHCR's 2012-13 recommendation to implement a cessation clause and lift the blanket refugee status conferred on approximately 4,000 Rwandan refugees who arrived in the country prior to 1999. The government stated it would not invoke the cessation clause while ambiguities concerning the local integration and permanent legal status for these long-term refugees remained unresolved. The government had yet to fully implement administrative processes for the naturalization of refugees who fell within the scope of the October 2015 Constitutional Court ruling, which allows long-staying refugees (in most cases, requiring more than 20 years' presence) to obtain citizenship through naturalization.

Access to Basic Services: Although the government granted refugees the same access as citizens to public health, education, and other services, there were anecdotal reports of discrimination against some refugees due to language barriers or xenophobia. The Refugee Commission of the Office of the Prime Minister, UNHCR, its implementing partners, and other NGOs worked to reduce barriers to access.

Durable Solutions: The government did not accept refugees for resettlement from foreign countries, but it facilitated UNHCR efforts to resettle refugees in foreign countries. The government assisted the safe and voluntary return of refugees to their homes.

Section 3. Freedom to Participate in the Political Process

The constitution and law provide citizens the ability to choose their government through free and fair periodic elections held by secret ballot and based on universal and equal suffrage. Nevertheless, the February 18 presidential and National Assembly elections were marred by serious irregularities.

Elections and Political Participation

<u>Recent Elections</u>: On February 18, the country held its fifth presidential and legislative elections since President Museveni came to power in 1986. The president was reelected with 61 percent of the vote, and FDC candidate Besigye finished second with 36 percent. The ruling NRM party captured approximately 70 percent of the seats in the 431-member unicameral National Assembly.

Domestic and international election observers stated that the elections fell short of international standards for credible democratic elections. The Commonwealth Observer Mission's report noted flawed processes, and the EU's report noted an atmosphere of intimidation and police use of excessive force against opposition supporters, media workers, and the general public. Domestic and international election observers noted biased media coverage and the Electoral Commission's (EC's) lack of transparency and independence.

Media reported voter bribery, multiple voting, ballot box stuffing, and the alteration of precinct and district results.

Late delivery of voting materials on election day, including ballots, disenfranchised many voters. The most significant delays--up to eight hours-- occurred in opposition-affiliated areas, including Kampala and Wakiso districts. While the EC extended voting from 4:00 p.m. to 7:00 p.m. at a number of polling stations that experienced delayed starts, officials at more than 30 of the most delayed stations cancelled voting and postponed it to the following day.

From February 19 to 29, the 10-day period during which opposition candidates could contest election results, police confined Besigye to his home and limited his access to lawyers and party leadership. Besigye's lawyers claimed police actions rendered it impossible for Besigye to file a legal challenge to election results, although Amama Mbabazi, who came third in the election, did challenge election results. On March 20, the Supreme Court upheld Museveni's victory, ruling that any incidents of noncompliance with electoral laws before and during the election process did not substantially affect results. On August 26, the Supreme Court recommended changes to electoral laws to increase fairness, including campaign finance reform and equal access for all candidates to state-owned media. The Supreme Court instructed the attorney general to report in two years on government implementation of reforms.

<u>Political Parties and Political Participation</u>: There were 29 registered parties, according to the EC. Security forces arbitrarily arrested and detained opposition leaders and intimidated and beat their supporters. While the ruling NRM party operated without restriction, regularly holding rallies and conducting political activities, authorities often prevented opposition parties and critical civil society organizations from organizing meetings or conducting activities. Authorities denied opposition parties access to media.

Domestic election observer groups, such as the Citizens' Coalition for Electoral Democracy, FHRI, and Citizens' Election Observers Network (CEON-U), reported authorities denied observers access to some stations and district tally centers. Security forces reportedly questioned the leaders of some groups after they released reports critical of the electoral process. In some districts resident district commissioners, who were the president's district level representatives, ordered accreditation committees to deny accreditation to CEON-U observers.

<u>Participation of Women and Minorities</u>: The law requires elections for seats reserved for special interest groups: 117 for women, five for labor, five for persons with disabilities, five for youth, and 10 for the UPDF. A single government-supported NGO organized an electoral college process that selected the five representatives for persons with disabilities.

Cultural factors limited women's political participation. CEON-U reported incidents of electoral intimidation in the Acholi, Rwenzori, Buganda, Karamoja, Teso, and Lango Regions that specifically targeted women. CEON-U also reported that amended laws to increase the fee required to nominate a candidate disproportionately affected women, who had less access to financial resources than their male counterparts. The law requires candidates seeking political public office to pay the government a nonrefundable nomination fee, which varied by position.

Section 4. Corruption and Lack of Transparency in Government

The 2009 Anticorruption Act provides criminal penalties for official corruption, including up to 12 years' imprisonment upon conviction. A 2015 amendment to the act mandates confiscation of the convicted persons' property. Nevertheless, the government did not implement the law effectively, and officials frequently engaged in corrupt practices with impunity. Government agencies responsible for combating corruption lacked the political will to combat corruption, particularly at the highest levels of government, and many corruption cases remained pending for years. Media reported numerous cases of government corruption during the year.

Police arrested and suspended several police officers implicated in bribery, extortion, and corruption cases. Authorities arrested several magistrates and judicial officials for forgery as well as for soliciting and receiving bribes.

The auditor general's annual audit findings for the fiscal year ending June 2015 concluded that the government flouted procurement rules, failed to implement internal controls, and spent funds without proper authorization.

Corruption: The 2015 audit report noted the government contravened procurement laws by directly procuring engineering and construction services to build two dams, valued at 7.7 trillion shillings ($2.2 billion), without an open international tender. The report also concluded the cost of the government's direct procurement of services for the construction of highways to the airport exceeded the market rate. According to the report, the government made more than 11 billion shillings ($3.1 million) in pension payments to beneficiaries whom the Ministry of Public Service could not confirm were alive.

On February 26, the Global Fund reported the government failed to account for $21.4 million (equivalent to 74.9 billion shillings) of donated medicines stored in government operated warehouses and that $2.4 million (equivalent to 8.4 billion shillings) worth of donated test kits issued to the government were not received by the targeted health facilities. It also reported the government could not account for $200,000 (equivalent to 700 million shillings) it generated from selling condoms that were meant to be distributed free of charge. Government officials reportedly sold Global Fund-subsidized antimalarial drugs for 50 percent more than the agreed price and did not account for the difference.

In August the DPP charged five suspects with diverting government resources, theft, forgery, and conspiracy to steal for diverting 15.4 billion shillings ($4.4 million) from a law firm that represented pensioners in a case against the government. Three of the suspects were also accused in the 2013 embezzlement case involving officials from the Ministries of Public Service and Finance; the officials allegedly embezzled more than 165 billion shillings ($47 million) from government pension funds by creating 2,605 ghost pensioners. In the case, eight officials were charged with corruption, but the court dismissed it in April 2015 after the state failed to present a witness after two years. In August 2015 the DPP reinstated the case and charged the same three officials with corruption for allegedly misappropriating 88 billion shillings ($25 million) in government funds. These cases continued at year's end.

On May 25, the Commission of Inquiry, which reports to the president, released the findings of its investigation into corruption in the Uganda National Roads Authority (UNRA). The inquiry revealed that UNRA officials misappropriated up to nine trillion shillings ($2.6 billion) from 2008 to 2015. The report noted "dramatic wheeling and dealing, insider trading and outright fraud." The report called for the prosecution of 90 officials and confiscation of their assets. The president ordered the inspector general of government (IGG), the director of the Criminal Investigations and Intelligence Department, police, and the Office of the Auditor General to conduct an investigation based on the report. On July 14, however, the High Court suspended the investigation due to a challenge of the report's findings issued by two construction firms, Dott Services Ltd. and General Nile Company for Roads and Bridges, which claimed their implication in the report was unfair and hurting their businesses. The case continued at year's end.

Financial Disclosure: Public officials are required to disclose their income, assets, and liabilities and those of their spouse, children, and dependents within three months after assuming office and every two years thereafter. The requirement applies to 42 position classifications, including ministers, MPs, leaders of political parties, judicial officers, permanent secretaries, and heads of government departments, among others. While these financial disclosures are officially considered public information, the IGG only released the records in response to a specific request. Public officials who vacate office six or more months after they declared their finances are required to refile as they conclude their term in office. The IGG is responsible for monitoring compliance; penalties include a warning or caution, demotion, dismissal, and administrative leave from office. According to Transparency International, most officials did not comply with disclosure requirements and those who did tended to underreport their assets.

Public Access to Information: The 2005 Access to Information (ATI) Act provides for public access to government information, but the law was not effectively implemented. According to The Hub for Investigative Media (HIM), a local NGO promoting government transparency, few citizens were aware of their right to public information, and government officials were often slow to respond, denied requests improperly, or did not respond at all. HIM has filed 39 cases against government departments that declined to provide information. The Africa Freedom of Information Center reported the government's $100,000 (equivalent to 350 million shillings) budget to implement the ATI was inadequate to train government officials and raise public awareness. The government could deny information requests based on security or sovereignty grounds, and the law provides for redress through internal dispute resolution processes or courts.

Section 5. Governmental Attitude Regarding International and Nongovernmental Investigation of Alleged Violations of Human Rights

Some domestic and international human rights groups operated without government restriction, investigating and publishing their findings on human rights cases. Authorities denied local LGBTI-related organizations official status due to discriminatory laws preventing their registration, however, and NGOs that worked in the areas of governance, human rights, and political participation were sometimes subject to extra scrutiny. The government was often unresponsive to concerns of local and international human rights organizations, and government officials often dismissed NGO claims of human rights abuses by security forces.

On March 4, for example, after NGOs criticized the arrests of journalists covering opposition protests, the police spokesperson dismissed the criticism as untrue, claiming the journalists were "obstructing police officers on duty and disobeying lawful orders."

In June HRAPF reported police refused to investigate a break-in at their office during which a private security guard was killed, although HRAPF provided police with television footage showing the intruders inside the office. Media reported a police spokesperson accused HRAPF management of "masterminding" the break-in.

The United Nations or Other International Bodies: In December 2015 the World Bank cancelled the Uganda Transport Sector Development Project, worth $265 million (equivalent to 927 billion shillings), due to the government's failure to address allegations of sexual misconduct and abuse by contractors with underage girls residing near the project site, sexual harassment of female employees, and child labor. The bank announced it would resume funding once the government established adequate measures to stop the abuses. In January, in response to the cancellation, President Museveni ordered the arrest of the project's government supervisors, although only low-level laborers had been charged with abuses by year's end. On May 16, media reported that the Fort Portal magistrate's court charged three persons with statutory rape. In June, after resuming the project with its own funds, the executive director of the National Roads Authority publicly warned such violations would not be tolerated and promised that his agency would closely monitor the project going forward. In May UNRA sponsored community training sessions on the protection of girls from labor exploitation and sexual abuse in the affected project areas.

<u>Government Human Rights Bodies</u>: The UHRC is a constitutionally mandated institution with quasi-judicial powers to investigate allegations of human rights abuses, direct the release of detainees, and award compensation to abuse victims. The president appoints its board, consisting of a chairperson and five commissioners. Unlike in the previous year, since February the UHRC had the necessary quorum of three commissioners to fulfill its duties; in that month the president reappointed three previous commissioners and appointed two new ones.

The UHRC, which had 21 branches nationwide, pursued suspected human rights abusers, including in the military and police forces. On August 1, the UHRC released its 2015 annual report, which noted 4,227 complaints, an increase of approximately 8 percent over 2014. For the sixth straight year, the highest number of complaints--more than 50 percent--were against the UPF; 13 percent of complaints were against the UPDF. The highest number of complaints involved torture and cruel, inhuman, or degrading treatment or punishment, followed by detention beyond 48 hours, child neglect, land disputes, and deprivation of life. The report also urged the Ministry of Justice and Constitutional Affairs to pay the more than five billion shillings ($1.43 million) in outstanding compensation awards owed to victims of human rights violations. Of the 579 million shillings ($165,000) awarded in 2015, most resulted from UPF violations, followed by those of the UPDF, and the UPF's Rapid Response Unit/Violent Crime Crack Unit.

Many human rights activists asserted the UHRC lacked the political will to investigate or identify senior-level perpetrators of abuses. Other observers commended the UHRC's 2015 report for the range of human rights problems identified and the report's recommendations, including that police adopt modern investigation techniques "to avoid [the] use of torture in obtaining information."

Section 6. Discrimination, Societal Abuses, and Trafficking in Persons

Women

<u>Rape and Domestic Violence</u>: The law criminalizes rape, which is punishable by life imprisonment or the death penalty; the law does not address spousal rape. The penal code defines rape as "unlawful carnal knowledge of a woman or a girl without her consent." Men accused of raping men are tried under section 145(a) of the penal code that prohibits "carnal knowledge of any person against the order of nature." The law also criminalizes domestic violence and provides up to two years' imprisonment for conviction.

Rape remained a serious problem throughout the country, and the government did not effectively enforce the law. Although the government arrested, prosecuted, and convicted persons for rape, the crime was seriously underreported, and police did not investigate most cases. The Center for Domestic Violence Protection (CEDOVIP) reported security officers often responded to women's claims of sexual violence with skepticism. Police lacked the criminal forensic capacity to collect evidence, which hampered prosecution and conviction. Although the law mandates police training on gender-based violence, training was often ad hoc and poorly attended, according to CEDOVIP.

The UPF crime report through June 2015, the most recent available, noted 10,163 reported sexual offenses, of which 787 were rapes, 8,954 statutory rapes, 308 indecent assaults, 56 incest, and 58 "unnatural offenses." Gulu District police told the media on April 1 they registered an average of 60 cases of statutory rape a month, with most cases involving girls younger than 14. According to the Uganda Association of Women Lawyers (FIDA), few cases involving rape and statutory rape were brought to trial and completed, in part due to societal factors. Parents, husbands, local leaders, religious leaders, police, prosecutors, and sometimes courts pressured victims to settle cases out of court. According to FIDA, these settlements often left perpetrators unpunished and discouraged other victims from seeking redress.

According to the 2011 Demographic and Health Survey (DHS), which the government conducted every five years, at least 27 percent of girls and women between the ages of 15 and 49 experienced some form of domestic violence in 2010. The same survey found at least 56 percent of married women reported some form of domestic violence. According to a representative from the UPF's Child and Family Protection Unit, victims often did not report domestic violence because society generally did not consider it a crime, and police officers often did not consider it a serious offense.

In 2015 local NGOs operated hotlines in 11 of the country's 112 districts. The government worked with local and international NGOs and religious institutions, including the Roman Catholic Church, to increase understanding of domestic violence as a human rights abuse. A few NGOs ran domestic violence shelters, including Action Aid, Mifumi, and Uganda Women's Network. Action Aid reported its shelters received between three and 10 domestic violence survivors daily. CEDOVIP operated a fund to provide victims of gender-based violence with emergency medical treatment, legal aid, transportation to police stations, and other services.

On August 17, the judiciary reported the introduction of audio/video link technology into the court system to enable vulnerable witnesses, especially children and victims of sexual assault, to testify without being in the same room as their alleged attacker. FIDA reported it was working with the judiciary to expedite gender-based violence cases through the court system by organizing special court sessions for victims.

On August 17, the cabinet passed a policy that requires the government to allocate funds to implement laws against gender-based violence, including the Domestic Violence Act of 2010, Prohibition of Female Genital Mutilation Act of 2010, and the Prevention of Trafficking in Persons Act of 2009. On November 25, the minister of gender, labor, and social development launched a five-year national action plan to eliminate gender-based violence, promote gender equality, and remove barriers to the advancement of women.

Female Genital Mutilation/Cutting (FGM/C): The law and constitution prohibit FGM/C of women and girls and establish a maximum penalty of 10 years' imprisonment for convicted perpetrators, or life imprisonment if the victim dies. UN Children's Fund (UNICEF) statistics updated in February showed 1 percent of women below the age of 50 had been subjected to FGM/C. The government, women's groups, and international organizations combated the practice through education and livelihood skills training. These programs, which received support from some local leaders, emphasized close cooperation with traditional authority figures and peer counseling. Nevertheless, the Sabiny and Pokot ethnic groups in the east along the Kenyan border continued the practice; the Sabiny practiced types I and II, and the Pokot practiced type III.

Local NGOs, including Reproductive Education and Community Health and the Kapchorwa Civil Organizations Alliance, held drama and theatrical plays in their communities to teach the legal provisions, penalties, and dangers associated with FGM/C. In December 2015, during the Sabiny's cultural day celebrations in Bukwo District, a delegation of Sabiny leaders led by Mzei Anguria Stephen, chairman of the Bukwo Elders Union, openly denounced FGM/C and urged the Sabiny people to shun the practice and educate their girls. In July, during the Pokot's annual cultural day in Amudat District, the district chairperson said local leaders had resolved to intensify the fight against FGM/C, which would save the lives of many young girls in the area. The UN Population Fund (UNFPA) collaborated with local churches to fight FGM/C.

Media reported on April 23 that pregnant women in eastern Kapchorwa District opted to give birth at home to avoid exposing themselves to health workers as having undergone FGM/C; this practice had the unfortunate consequence of increased infant and maternal mortality rates in the district.

Other Harmful Traditional Practices: Media reported several cases of ritual child killings. Kyampisi Childcare Ministries reported in February that six children were mutilated and killed during the election season as part of rituals to bring good fortune to political candidates. The Coordination Office to Combat Trafficking in Persons reported nine victims of ritual killings through June.

On May 25, police arrested Herbert Were after they found him with his eight-year-old brother's head. Police said Were confessed to beheading his brother as a precondition for joining a cult named "illuminati," which promised he would become wealthy.

Sexual Harassment: The law criminalizes sexual harassment and provides for penalties of up to 14 years' imprisonment, but authorities did not effectively enforce the law. Sexual harassment was a serious and widespread problem in homes, schools, universities, and workplaces. The Ministry of Gender, Labor, and Social Development (MGLSD) reported that fear of retaliation deterred many victims from reporting harassment.

Reproductive Rights: Couples and individuals have the right to decide the number, spacing, and timing of their children, manage their reproductive health, and have access to the information and means to do so, free from coercion, discrimination, or violence; however, family planning information and assistance were difficult to access, particularly in rural areas, where there were few health clinics. According to the 2011 DHS, one in three married women wanted to delay childbirth or space their children but could not access family planning aids. During the year the Ministry of Health reported that 36 percent of women between the ages of 15 to 49 used contraception. Women also faced challenges of religious restrictions imposed by faiths that oppose contraception.

Men's lack of support for, or active opposition to, family planning often was a main deterrent to contraceptive use, according to a study conducted during the year by the NGO Coalition for Health Promotion and Social Development. In August the spokesperson for the government-run National Medical Stores reported men often harassed and beat their wives for using contraceptives.

According to the World Health Organization, the country's maternal mortality rate was 343 per 100,000 live births. Health officials attributed the high maternal mortality rate to medical complications during delivery and the inability of healthcare facilities to manage them; media cited staff shortages and inadequate supplies at healthcare centers, also noting that health-care centers in rural communities often were inaccessible. According to UNFPA, only 57 percent of births were attended by skilled healthcare personnel.

In June 2015 the Ministry of Health established standards and guidelines to reduce morbidity and mortality related to unsafe abortions, including increasing access to family planning services and legal postabortion care and services. Fear of arrest often made healthcare professionals unwilling to attend to women who had undergone an abortion because the service providers feared police would accuse them of having performed the abortion. Abortion is a criminal offense and punishable by up to 14 years' imprisonment for the practitioner and seven years for the mother.

<u>Discrimination</u>: The law provides women the same legal status and rights as men. Discrimination against women, however, was widespread, especially in rural areas. Local NGOs reported numerous cases of discrimination against women in divorce, employment, owning or managing businesses and property, education, and other areas. Many customary laws discriminate against women in adoption, marriage, divorce, and inheritance. Under local customary law in many areas, women may not own or inherit property or retain custody of their children. Traditional divorce law in many areas requires women to meet stricter evidentiary standards than men to prove adultery. Polygyny is legal under both customary and Islamic law. In some ethnic groups, men may "inherit" the widows of their deceased brothers.

During the year CEDOVIP reported receiving 18 cases concerning widows whose in-laws denied them access to marital property, housing, and their children, particularly in cases where the women's names were absent from the property documents and when the women were in polygynous relationships. The law does not recognize cohabiting relationships, and women involved in such relationships had no judicial recourse to protect their rights.

The law provides that "every employer shall pay males and females equal remuneration for work of equal value." In 2013 the National Organization of

Trade Unions (NOTU) reported, however, that women received much lower wages than men for the same work.

Children

Birth Registration: The law accords citizenship to children born in or outside the country if at least one parent or grandparent is a citizen at the time of birth. Abandoned children under the age of 18 with no known parents are considered citizens, as are children under the age of 18 adopted by citizens.

The law requires citizens to register a birth within three months. The National Identification and Registration Authority, established in 2015, is responsible for registering all persons in the country for the purpose of national identification. According to the 2011 DHS, only 29 percent of rural and 38 percent of urban births were registered. Lack of birth registration generally did not result in denial of public services. Some primary schools, however, required birth certificates for enrollment, especially those in urban centers. Enrollment in public secondary schools, university, and tertiary institutions required birth certificates.

Education: The government provided free universal primary education to four children per family as well as universal secondary education, although parents were required to provide lunch and schooling materials for children in secondary school.

A 2015 International Center for Research on Women study indicated more than 50 percent of girls between the ages of 14 and 18 dropped out of school due to poverty and early pregnancy. The government reported significantly higher dropout rates for girls than boys, due to early pregnancy, child marriages, sexual harassment and abuse, lack of access to sanitary pads, and poverty.

Child Abuse: Child abuse remained a serious problem. Authorities maintained a national hotline to report child abuse and received 4,891 reports between June 2014 and August 2015. Adolescent children were particularly vulnerable to sexual exploitation, early marriage, human trafficking, drug and substance abuse, involvement in social unrest, and engaging in criminal activities. From January through June 2015, the most recent data available, police registered 7,349 child related offenses, including 4,430 cases of child neglect, 1,366 of abandonment, 755 of abuse, 674 kidnappings (enticing a minor from a guardian) and abductions (forcing a minor away from a guardian), 76 cases of trafficking, and 48 of infanticide.

The law considers sexual contact outside marriage with children under the age of 18, regardless of consent or age of the perpetrator, as "statutory rape," which carries a maximum penalty of death. Payment to the child's parents often settled such cases. In September 2015 IGP Mugenyi said statutory rape was the most common crime against children. In 2013 the Ministry of Education and Sports and UNICEF released a study indicating 78 percent of primary school children and 82 percent of secondary students had experienced sexual abuse. In most cases the perpetrators were teachers. Of the victims, only 40 percent of girls and 39 percent of boys reported the abuse to authorities.

The government continued to work with UNICEF and NGOs--including Save the Children, Child Fund, and the African Network for the Prevention and Protection against Child Abuse and Neglect (ANPPCAN)--to combat child abuse. The UPF provided free rape and statutory rape medical examination kits to hospitals and medical practitioners throughout the country to assist investigations.

Corporal punishment is illegal, but remained a problem in schools and sometimes resulted in permanent injuries. On May 20, the president signed the 2015 Children Amendment Act, which makes corporal punishment in schools punishable by up to three years' imprisonment. The amendment also seeks to protect children from hazardous employment and harmful traditional practices, including child marriage and FGM/C.

Early and Forced Marriage: The legal minimum age for marriage is 18, but authorities generally did not enforce the law. Marriage of underage girls by parental arrangement was common in rural areas. In 2015 local NGOs and the police's Family and Children Unit reported some parents arranged marriages or other sexual arrangements for girls as young as 12. UNICEF's 2016 *State of the World's Children* report estimated 10 percent of the country's girls married before the age of 15 and 40 percent were married by the age of 18.

On January 6, media reported police arrested seven persons in Jinja District for allegedly attempting to marry a 14-year-old girl to a 19-year-old man.

Female Genital Mutilation/Cutting: See information for girls under the age of 18 in the women's section above.

Sexual Exploitation of Children: While the law prohibits sexual exploitation of children, the government did not enforce the law effectively, and the problem was extensive. The minimum age for consensual sex is 18. Statutory rape, which refers to any sexual contact with a minor, carries a maximum penalty of death. Victims' parents, however, often opted to settle cases out of court for a payment. The law prohibits child pornography.

The 2011 Computer Misuse Act carries a definition of child pornography that adheres to international legal standards, but the act does not specifically address the solicitation of children for sexual purposes.

Child prostitution remained a problem. The National Information Technology Authority (NITA) reported an increase in the number of child sex abuse cases, noting the internet makes it easier for pedophiles to target children online. The Ministry of Internal Affairs conducted several training sessions for police officers on combatting online child abuse, and NITA reported it established a portal on its website to receive complaints of online child sexual abuse and child pornography. The local NGO Uganda Youth Development Link estimated in 2015 that at least 18,000 girls and women engaged in sex work across the country.

Child Soldiers: In July Katumba Wamala, army commander and chief of defense forces, warned that the rebel Allied Democratic Forces recruited child soldiers, particularly in the east.

The Lord's Resistance Army continued to hold women and children against their will and to abduct children from neighboring countries.

Infanticide or Infanticide of Children with Disabilities: From January to June 2015, the most recent information available, the UPF reported 48 infanticides.

Displaced Children: Families in the remote Karamoja Region sent many children to Kampala during the dry season to find work and beg on the streets. In March the International Human Trafficking Institute reported that some Karamojong parents sent their children to Kampala with recruiters who promised to find them work but instead forced them to beg on the streets. A 2015 study by ANPPCAN found that 57 percent of Kampala's street children were from Karamoja.

Police routinely rounded up street children and relocated them to a custodial home for juvenile delinquents, where staff attempted to locate the children's families and return them to their homes. Media reported police often found that children who had been returned to their families reappeared on Kampala's streets soon thereafter. In April the MGLSD reported the government completed and opened a rehabilitation institution in Karamoja to assist Karamojong children.

Institutionalized Children: There were reports of abuses in several orphanages. For example, on April 8, media reported that police closed an illegal orphanage in Lwengo District that housed 26 children in three rooms, denied them food for several days, and prevented them from going to school.

According to regulations issued in 2014, an approved orphanage "shall only receive children in an emergency from a police officer or under an interim care order from a judge." All approved homes are required to keep proper accounts, employ a qualified warden and registered nurse, keep health records for each child, provide adequate sleeping facilities, and provide for an appropriate education. Nevertheless, the government lacked the resources to register and monitor orphanages.

In 2015 the MGLSD estimated there were more than 50,000 children in approximately 1,000 orphanages in the country, of which only 83 were licensed by the ministry. More than half of the orphanages did not meet minimal standards and held children illegally. Nearly 70 percent of orphanages maintained inadequate records on the children present. Most children in orphanages had at least one living parent.

International Child Abductions: The country is not a party to the 1980 Hague Convention on the Civil Aspects of International Child Abduction. See the Department of State's *Annual Report on International Parental Child Abduction* at travel.state.gov/content/childabduction/en/legal/compliance.html.

Anti-Semitism

The Jewish community had approximately 2,000 members centered in Mbale District, in the eastern part of the country. There were no reports of anti-Semitic acts.

Trafficking in Persons

See the Department of State's *Trafficking in Persons Report* at www.state.gov/j/tip/rls/tiprpt/.

Persons with Disabilities

The law prohibits discrimination against persons with physical, sensory, intellectual, or mental disabilities in employment, education, air travel and other transportation, access to health care, the judicial system, or the provision of other state services. The law, however, does not establish penalties for those engaging in discrimination. The law provides for access to all buildings "where the public is invited" and information and communications for persons with disabilities, but the government did not enforce the law effectively. A 2013 study conducted by architects in Kampala found that 95 percent of the city's buildings were inaccessible to persons with disabilities due to lack of ramps or elevators.

Persons with disabilities faced societal discrimination and very limited job and educational opportunities. The UHRC received complaints of discrimination in employment (see section 7.d.) and access to transport and other public services.

Most schools did not accommodate persons with disabilities.

In June Plan International reported many children with disabilities were victims of physical and emotional abuse, including bullying, ridicule, and social isolation. Perpetrators included parents, foster parents, and teachers as well as peers. Plan International reported that 84 percent of children with disabilities had been victims of violence, compared with 54 percent of children without disabilities. A 2012 report released by the National Council on Disability (NCD), the most recent information available, indicated 45 percent of persons with disabilities were literate, compared with 71 percent in the general population. The report found children with mental disabilities were sometimes denied food and tied to trees and beds with ropes to control their movements.

The government took steps during the year to address the needs of persons with disabilities. The government increased fiscal year 2016 funding by 34 percent for training teachers working with children with special needs. The Mukono District Council passed a resolution that banned the construction of buildings that do not have provisions of access for persons living with disabilities.

In July the National Union of Disabled Persons of Uganda petitioned the chief justice to improve access to courthouses for persons with disabilities and to introduce sign language and Braille systems in the courts.

The law reserves five seats in the National Assembly for representatives of persons with disabilities. The NCD reported participation by persons with disabilities in the February elections was minimal, in part due to inaccessibility of polling centers. Election materials were not modified for persons with vision disabilities, and polling stations lacked support services such as guides, helpers, and sign language interpreters. The NCD also noted civic education offered by the government to citizens through electronic and print media was inaccessible to many persons with disabilities.

Government agencies responsible for protecting the rights of persons with disabilities, including the Ministry of State for Disabled Persons under the MGLSD and the NCD, lacked sufficient funding to undertake significant initiatives.

National/Racial/Ethnic Minorities

There were reports of violence among ethnic minorities over land, grazing rights, border demarcations, and other contested matters.

On July 15, the international NGO Human Rights Watch (HRW) reported that during a March 11-25 operation to quell interethnic violence between the Bamba and Bakonzo tribes, the UPDF and UPF shot and killed 17 civilians in Bundibugyo and Kasese Districts. According to HRW, 13 of the civilians were unarmed. A police spokesperson claimed security forces were responding to attacks with machetes and stones. The National Assembly's Defense and Internal Affairs Committee launched an investigation, but no report had been released by year's end.

On February 8, media reported a group of citizens and residents of foreign extraction complained of discrimination in the process of applying for national identity cards. The group, called the Uganda Multiracial Community, alleged the Ministry of Internal Affairs denied some of its members, citizens and noncitizens, official registration. Yasin Omar, the group's head, said that some persons of multiracial backgrounds paid up to 500,000 shillings ($142) to obtain identity cards, although the government was supposed to issue them without charge. The president met the group in February and promised to resolve their problems with the Ministry of Internal Affairs. No further update was available.

Indigenous People

The constitution recognizes 56 indigenous ethnicities. The government has historically displaced indigenous groups to create national parks and reserves.

Unlike in previous years, media did not report any clashes between the Benet ethnic group, evicted from its land on Mount Elgon in 1983, and the Uganda Wildlife Authority. It was unknown whether the government had fully complied with a 2005 ruling that returned lands within Mount Elgon to the Benet.

Unlike in previous years, there were no known reports of neighboring communities discriminating against the Batwa ethnic group, which the government displaced in 1992 when it created Mgahinga National Park, Bwindi Impenetrable National Park, and Echuya Central Forest Reserve. Conflict in previous years resulted from resentment by local ethnic groups residing in the area where the government resettled the Batwa.

Acts of Violence, Discrimination, and Other Abuses Based on Sexual Orientation and Gender Identity

Consensual same-sex sexual conduct is illegal according to a colonial era law that criminalizes "carnal knowledge of any person against the order of nature" and provides for a penalty of up to life imprisonment. LGBTI persons faced discrimination, legal restrictions, societal harassment and violence, intimidation, and threats.

On August 4, police raided an LGBTI pride week event at a Kampala nightclub and ordered the approximately 300 attendees to huddle in a corner and sit on the floor. There were multiple reports police beat other attendees who hid in the club's bathrooms or attempted to exit the club. There were also reports police sexually assaulted transgender individuals. According to witnesses, police ordered the event organizers to come forward, arrested 16 individuals without charge, and kept them for several hours in a holding cell, where police incited other detainees in the cell to beat them.

In a separate case, the LGBTI community cancelled a pride week parade event after the minister for ethics and integrity, Simon Lokodo, threatened to mobilize civilians to beat participants. The minister then released a statement saying LGBTI activities were criminal and illegal. The minister, who later denied the threat, claimed police cancelled the event because organizers had failed to obtain prior police permission, a claim HRW disputed.

In 2015 the Uganda Registration Service Bureau (URSB) rejected the application of Sexual Minorities Uganda (SMUG) to reserve its name, the first step required to register as an NGO. As explanation for its refusal, the URSB cited the 2012 Companies Act that allows it to refuse any requested name that "in the opinion of the registrar is undesirable." On June 1, SMUG, with support from HRAPF, filed a suit claiming the URSB's decision violated the organization's constitutional rights to associate and assemble. The case continued at year's end.

In January 2015 police arrested nine men who helped organize an HIV/AIDS testing clinic in the western Ntungamo District for "carnal knowledge against the order of nature." Police claimed four of those arrested were engaged in sexual activity at the time of arrest, a charge disputed by those arrested. The men, who were subjected to forced anal exams, were released on bond. The case continued at year's end.

HIV and AIDS Social Stigma

Although the law prohibits discrimination against persons with HIV/AIDS, discrimination was common and prevented persons with HIV/AIDS from obtaining treatment and support. International and local NGOs, in cooperation with the government, sponsored public awareness campaigns to eliminate the stigma of HIV/AIDS. Counselors encouraged clients to be tested and to receive information about HIV/AIDS with their partners and family. Persons with HIV/AIDS formed support groups to promote awareness in their communities.

Police and the UPDF regularly refused to recruit persons who tested positive for HIV, claiming their bodies would be too weak for rigorous training and subsequent deployment.

In 2014 the National Assembly passed the HIV and AIDS Prevention and Control Bill that creates a legal framework for the prevention and control of HIV, disclosure of seropositive status to reduce transmissions, testing and counseling services, and prescribes penalties for the intentional spread of HIV. In July 2015 the president signed the bill into law. Human rights and HIV/AIDS activists criticized the bill, asserting it represented a dangerous backslide in the country's effort to respond to HIV. Activists expressed concern about a clause in the bill that criminalizes attempted and intentional transmission of HIV. A person convicted of these offenses faces up to 10 years' imprisonment or a fine of approximately five million shillings ($1,430).

In September the International Community of Women Living with HIV Eastern Africa reported the results of research in 2014-15 indicating that healthcare workers sterilized 72 women living with HIV without their consent between 1993 and 2013. Most of the cases took place in government-run hospitals during childbirth by caesarian section.

Other Societal Violence or Discrimination

Mob violence remained a problem. Mobs attacked and killed persons suspected of robbery, killing, rape, theft, ritual sacrifice, and witchcraft, among other crimes. Mobs beat, lynched, burned, and otherwise brutalized their victims.

On March 22, media reported that motorcycle taxi drivers organized an illegal court in Lugazi, which tried, sentenced to death, and subsequently beat to death a man accused of stealing a motorcycle.

Section 7. Worker Rights

a. Freedom of Association and the Right to Collective Bargaining

The law allows workers, except members of the armed forces, to form and join independent unions, bargain collectively, and take industrial action. Unions must obtain a document of recognition before engaging in collective bargaining. Employers who violate a worker's right to form and join a trade union or bargain collectively may face up to four years' imprisonment and a fine of 1.9 million shillings ($542).

The law allows unions to conduct activities without interference, prohibits antiunion discrimination by employers, and provides for reinstatement of workers dismissed for union activity. The law also empowers the minister of gender, labor, and social development and labor officers to refer disputes to the Industrial Court if initial mediation and arbitration attempts fail.

The government did not effectively enforce applicable labor laws. MGLSD officials said their ministry was inadequately funded and failed to undertake sufficient labor inspections. Penalties were generally not adequate to deter violations.

The government generally did not respect the constitutionally guaranteed rights to freedom of association and collective bargaining, and the government did not always protect these rights. Labor activists reported some employers avoided the legal requirement to enter into collective bargaining agreements with registered unions by subcontracting and outsourcing services. NOTU reported some employers used a "recognition agreement" to allow union operations at the workplace. Most employers did not provide their employees written employment contracts, resulting in a lack of job security and union representation.

Trade associations were independent of the government and political parties, but MPs who held the five National Assembly seats reserved for workers tended to be affiliated with a political party (currently four were members of the ruling NRM party and the fifth was unaffiliated). To register, trade unions must submit an application to the registrar of unions, including copies of the union's constitution, rules, address, list of members, employees, and a registration fee. The registrar should grant a certificate of registration within 90 days of receiving a completed application. In November 2015 the National Assembly passed the Parliamentary Elections (Amendment) (No. 2) Bill, which for the first time allowed nonunionized workers to vote for their representatives in the National Assembly.

On August 1, nearly 4,000 nonteaching staff members at five of the country's six public universities began a 17-day sit-down strike. The nonteaching staff demanded back pay amounting to 56 billion shillings ($16 million) and a salary increase. The strike delayed the start of the academic year by more than two weeks. Describing the strike as a sign of indiscipline and lack of professional ethics, the president vowed on August 14 that the government would not give strikers a raise. Two days later, following a meeting with the Public Universities Nonteaching Staff Executives Forum, Museveni promised to pay the salary arrears by December, ending the strike. The government had not paid the promised salary arrears by year's end.

Antiunion discrimination occurred, and labor activists accused several companies of preventing employees from joining unions by denying promotions, not renewing work contracts, and sometimes refusing to recognize unions. NOTU officials reported many workers were discouraged from joining trade unions due to fear of harassment and dismissal.

Public service unions, including medical staff and teachers, were able to negotiate salaries and employment terms for members. The government fixed salaries for "essential government employees," including police, military, and management level officials.

b. Prohibition of Forced or Compulsory Labor

The law prohibits forced or compulsory labor, including by children, but does not prohibit prison labor. The law states that prison labor would only be considered forced labor if a worker is "hired out to, or placed at the disposal of, a private individual, company, or association." Those convicted of forced labor may be fined up to 960,000 shillings ($274), sentenced to two years' imprisonment, or both, and required to pay a fine of 80,000 shillings ($23) "for each day the compulsory labor continued."

The government's Anti-Human Trafficking Task Force (AHTTF) and the MGLSD reported that many citizens working overseas, particularly in the Arab Persian Gulf States, became victims of forced labor. In January the government announced a three-month ban on its citizens' working as domestic workers in Saudi Arabia in response to growing concerns over human rights abuse of these workers in the country. The ban, which was initially intended to allow the MGLSD time to investigate the problem, remained in effect at year's end, despite the MGLSD's September 22 announcement that it had completed the investigation and would lift the ban. According to the MGLSD investigation, none of the victims of forced labor and sexual exploitation had been recruited by registered companies. The MGLSD reported there were 53 registered recruitment companies, 34 of which belonged to the Uganda Association of External Recruitment Agencies. The minister also announced that the MGLSD was drafting stringent regulations to control citizens' labor migration and protect them from labor exploitation. According to media reports, the recruitment of domestic workers continued largely unabated due largely to the government's poor enforcement of the ban. The AHTTF reported the government did not have funds to investigate cases abroad and relied on assistance from civil society to repatriate citizens.

In 2015 FHRI noted cases of forced labor in 23 of the 31 prisons it inspected. In addition persons held in pretrial detention often were subjected to forced labor. Prison officials allegedly hired out prisoners to work on private farms and construction sites. Male prisoners tended to do arduous physical labor, while female prisoners often produced marketable handicrafts, such as woven baskets. When paid, compensation was generally very low. On April 12, a mayor in Lwengo District publicly denounced the practice of hiring out prisoners to work on private farms and accused prison wardens of stealing their wages.

Also see the Department of State's *Trafficking in Persons Report* at www.state.gov/j/tip/rls/tiprpt/.

c. Prohibition of Child Labor and Minimum Age for Employment

The law bars children younger than 12 from doing any work, but allows employers to hire children younger than 16 to do work the law defines as "nonhazardous," such as domestic work, if it does not interfere with the child's education. MGLSD regulations prohibit children between the ages of 15 and 17 from working overtime (more than 48 hours a week). The law prohibits children working from 7 p.m. to 7 a.m. or from being employed in work that is "injurious to their health, dangerous or hazardous or otherwise unsuitable." The law provides for government inspection of workplaces, identification of workplace hazards, and other related matters for all workers, including children. Violations of child labor laws carry a 685,055 shilling ($195) fine. There were no known convictions under the law since its adoption in 2006. Children's rights activists reported the employment of children as young as five.

Institutions responsible for enforcing child labor laws and policies included the National Council of Children, the police Child and Family Protection Unit, the Industrial Court, and the MGLSD. The government's enforcement of applicable laws was ineffective due to understaffing, lack of funding, insufficient training, and weak interagency coordination mechanisms, according to NOTU. MGLSD officials acknowledged financial constraints limited enforcement efforts. The ministry, in conjunction with civil society, provided social services to children working in the worst forms of child labor and other vulnerable groups and conducted training sessions for some staff members, local leaders, and district labor inspectors. MGLSD labor officers conducted inspections and reported child labor problems to the minister; however, more than half the country's 117 districts were without a labor officer. In some districts without labor officers, district community development officers (CDOs) doubled as labor officers, although these CDOs had no additional funding to support labor functions. Due to lack of funds and logistical support, district labor officials have not conducted any inspections exclusively for child labor since 2004.

The government coordinated its efforts to stop child labor through the National Steering Committee on Child Labor, which included representatives of the MGLSD, the Ministry of Education and Sports, the Ministry of Local Government, the Ministry of Agriculture, and the Ministry of Health. Other organizations represented included the National Council for Children, the UPF's Child and Family Protection Unit, the Federation of Uganda Employers, NOTU, the Central

Organization of Free Trade Unions, the Uganda National Teachers' Union, NGOs, journalists, and academics.

The government cooperated with the International Labor Organization, foreign governments, and NGOs on several initiatives to combat child labor, including education and reintegration of child laborers into their communities. Several human rights NGOs continued programs to remove children from hazardous work situations, including commercial sexual exploitation and domestic work, among others.

Child labor was common, especially in the informal sector. Child labor predominantly occurred in cattle herding, transport, gold mining, street vending, begging, scrap collecting, stone quarrying, brick making, road construction and repair, car washing, fishing, domestic services, bar or club service work, cross-border smuggling, and commercial farming (including the production of tea, coffee, sugarcane, vanilla, tobacco, rice, cotton, charcoal, and palm oil). In urban areas, children sold small items on the street, worked in shops, begged for money, and were exploited in the commercial sex industry. Multiple reports found children engaged in gold mining sometimes worked during school breaks, after classes, and on weekends. In some cases children worked full time and did not attend school. Many children left school and engaged in agricultural or domestic work to help meet expenses or perform the work of absent or sick parents, a common situation throughout the country. The problem was particularly acute among the large orphan population. According to UNICEF's 2016 *State of the World's Children* report, 16 percent of the country's children between the ages of five and 14 were engaged in child labor.

In December 2015 the World Bank cancelled the Uganda Transport Sector Development Project, worth $265 million (equivalent to 927 billion shillings), after allegations of misconduct and abuse by contractors, including child labor.

Also see the Department of Labor's *Findings on the Worst Forms of Child Labor* at www.dol.gov/ilab/reports/child-labor/findings/.

d. Discrimination with Respect to Employment and Occupation

The constitution and employment laws prohibit discrimination based on race, sex, religion, political opinion, national origin or citizenship, social origin, disability, age, language, and HIV/communicable disease status; however, the law does not address sexual orientation or gender identity. There were cases of employment

discrimination based on these categories. In June the local NGO Platform for
Labor Action, which focuses on workers' rights, reported some employers forced
their domestic staff to undergo HIV testing and fired those who tested positive.

e. Acceptable Conditions of Work

The legal minimum wage was set in 1984 at 6,000 shillings ($1.71) per month. In
2003 the government and the private sector agreed in principle to increase the
minimum wage to 54,000 shillings ($15.42) per month. The government has yet to
implement this agreement. In May 2015 the president argued against setting a
minimum wage, claiming it would undermine investment by increasing labor costs.
In June 2015 the government established the Minimum Wages Advisory Board
consisting of representatives from the government, workers, and employers to
assess the feasibility of a minimum wage. In May the permanent secretary of the
MGLSD reported that the advisory board had submitted its preliminary findings to
the president's office and ministers, but did not release them publicly.

In September the World Bank released a poverty assessment report for 2006-13
that indicated 35 percent of the population lived below the international poverty
line of $1.90 (equivalent to 6,650 shillings) a day while 20 percent lived below the
national poverty line, which ranged from $0.88 (equivalent to 3,080 shillings) to
$1.04 (equivalent to 3,640 shillings) a day.

The legal maximum workweek is 48 hours, and the maximum workday is 10
hours. The law provides that the workweek may be extended to 56 hours per
week, including overtime, with the employee's consent. An employee may work
more than 10 hours in a single day if the average number of hours over a period of
three weeks does not exceed 10 hours per day, or 56 hours per week. For
employees who work beyond 48 hours in a single week, the law requires
employers to pay a minimum of 1.5 times the employee's normal hourly rate for
the overtime hours, and twice the employee's normal hourly rate for work on
public holidays. The law grants employees a 30-minute break during every eight-
hour work shift. For every four months of continuous employment, an employee is
entitled to seven days of paid annual leave. Many industries paid workers annual
bonuses in lieu of overtime.

The law establishes occupational safety and health standards and regulations for all
workers, enforced by the MGLSD's Department of Occupational Safety and
Health. The law provides labor inspectors authority to access and examine any
workplace and prosecute suspected violators of the law. Labor officials conducted

desk reviews and site inspections to assess compliance with safety and health standards in several sectors, including the production of beer and other beverages, sugar processing, and steel manufacturing.

Authorities did not effectively enforce labor laws. The MGLSD mainly conducted labor inspections in response to complaints. Only 49 of the country's 117 districts had a labor officer, and their training, funding, and logistical support were inadequate. The MGLSD reported that it conducted more than 100 on-site inspections, 120 desk reviews, and 50 routine inspections during the year. In some of the districts without labor officers, community development officers assumed this responsibility. Community development officers are local officials responsible for supervising government-funded development programs. While such individuals are supposed to conduct labor inspections, they lacked the training and often only addressed labor issues reported to them. As a result, the Department of Occupational Safety and Health carried out some site inspections during the year. NOTU officials claimed the government favored investors over workers, making it difficult for labor inspectors to enforce the law. Labor officials reported the labor law does not protect workers in the informal, domestic, and agricultural sectors.

On April 25, media outlets reported the Federation of Ugandan Employers (FUE) conducted a one-day training session on the country's labor laws for the Chinese companies in the country. At the training session, FUE distributed a simplified guide on labor laws, translated into Chinese. According to the embassy of China in Kampala, Chinese companies employed an estimated 20,000 persons, mainly in construction, television assembly, fabrication of plastic products, oil exploration, and woodworking.

NOTU officials reported that, due to the country's high unemployment rate, which the 2014 National Census report estimated at 9.4 percent, and underemployment rate, which the Bureau of Statistics reported at 12.9 percent in 2015, employers had disproportionate power to determine employees' salaries. Sometimes employers paid workers as little as 50,000 shillings ($14.25) per month. Workers often were subjected to hazardous working conditions. Violations of standard wages, overtime pay, or safety and health standards were common in several sectors, including steel fabrication, factory work, domestic work, and the informal sector.

On June 16, the Uganda Retirement Benefits Regulatory Authority (URBRA) licensed the country's retirement programs for the informal sector. The new programs cover traders and individuals engaged in various forms of informal work. Figures released by the Bureau of Statistics in 2014 estimated the informal sector produced 49 percent of the country's gross domestic product and employed up to 80 percent of the labor force. URBRA reported most of the country's 13 million eligible workers were in the informal and agricultural sectors. The formal pension systems cover less than 10 percent of the working population.

Deaths occurred due to unsafe working environments. For example, media outlets reported in December 2015 that two staff members working at a copper mine died in separate incidents, one crushed by the factory's conveyor drum and another by an underground copper carrier. The MGLSD and civil society reported that, due to the high unemployment rate and rate of informal labor, workers felt compelled to remain in work situations that endangered their health, and feared reprisals if they demanded improved conditions. The government did not effectively protect employees in these situations, due to insufficient legislation and resources for monitoring mechanisms.

www.ingramcontent.com/pod-product-compliance
Lightning Source LLC
Chambersburg PA
CBHW081253250726
48654CB00012B/1591